Exiles of Eden

Exiles of Eden

Ladan Osman

COFFEE HOUSE PRESS

Minneapolis

2019

Coffee House Press books are available to the trade through our primary distributor, Consortium Book Sales & Distribution, cbsd.com or (800) 283-3572. For personal orders, catalogs, or other information, write to info@coffeehousepress.org.

Coffee House Press is a nonprofit literary publishing house. Support from private foundations, corporate giving programs, government programs, and generous individuals helps make the publication of our books possible. We gratefully acknowledge their support in detail in the back of this book.

LIBRARY OF CONGRESS CATALOGING-IN-PUBLICATION DATA

Names: Osman, Ladan, author.
Title: Exiles of Eden / Ladan Osman.
Description: Minneapolis : Coffee House Press, [2019]
Identifiers: LCCN 2018040459 (print) | LCCN 2018041999 (ebook) |
    ISBN 9781566895538 (ebook) | ISBN 9781566895446 (trade pbk.)
Classification: LCC PS3615.S53 (ebook) | LCC PS3615.S53 A6 2019 (print) |
    DDC 811/.6—dc23
LC record available at https://lccn.loc.gov/2018040459

PRINTED IN THE UNITED STATES OF AMERICA

26 25 24 23 22 21 20 19   1 2 3 4 5 6 7 8

For Brigit Pegeen Kelly
1951–2016

the dead can mother nothing ... nothing
but our sight
—"Dead Doe: I"

Contents

to have a home is not a favour

—"Anguish Longer Than Sorrow,"
Keorapetse Kgositsile (1938–2018)

Exiles of Eden

I

Half-Life

Don't turn a scientific problem into a common love story.
　—*Solaris* (1972)

How can I fail outside and inside our home? I decay in our half-life.
How can I fail with my body? How do I stay alone in this half-life?
I started a ghazal about my hope's stress fracture.
I require rest from your unfocused eyes, my heat,
which is becoming objective and observable.
A friend asks, "What are you waiting for?
The straw that breaks the camel's back?"
Maybe I am the straw.
Maybe I am hay. I made a list of rhyming words:
bray, flay, array.
They relate to farms, decaying things,
gray days, dismay.
I am recently reckless about making a display
of my unhappiness. Perhaps you may survey it.
Perhaps I may stray from it, go to the wrong home
by accident and say, "Oh! Here already?"
You know I'm fraying.
You don't try to braid me together.
You don't notice a tomcat wiggling his hind legs,
ready to gather all my fabric,
his paws over my accidental tassels.
I've learned how to be appropriate sitting on my hands
on the couch, not allowed to touch you.
"Sex?" you say, like I asked you to make a carcass our shelter.

I don't recount my dreams to you
because you're insulted in most of them.
Remember when I asked you to break into a building?
"Let's have an adventure, any."
I dreamed another man was taking me into a locked school.

"Let's go," he said. No face, his hand straight behind him.
He was wearing a black peacoat.
Many men wear black wool coats. You have one.
Hell, I have one. I may have been leading myself.

"How long will you live this half-life?"
my mother asks during a phone call when, so absent
of any particular emotion, I couldn't catch my breath.
She thought I was upset, losing my temper in the street.
It's months later, and when we talk
she says, "I was so happy today. Does that make sense?
And here I am, sleeping on a bed older than your baby sister."
I'm not sure what bothers me but my voice gets low
and I repeat myself.
I raise and drop my palate without sound.
"Good-night," we say, each with something unaddressed,
without allay.

I try to remember half-lives, learned in science rooms,
air dense with iron, vinegar. The process of dating old bones,
old stones. Unstable nuclei, decay by two or more processes.
Exponential death, exponential halving of a life.
My mother has given me something to pursue and solve.
I study the internet:
"The biological half-life of water in a human being is about
7 to 14 days, though this can be altered by his/her behavior."
This makes me want to fall asleep in the bathtub.
In this house, it's how we escape each other,
where we find another warm body, moisture,
work a sweat on our brows.

I search *doubling time,* a related term,
because I hate feeling fractioned.
Kitchens, bowls of water steaming under dough:
How long will it take to grow to twice its size?

Depends on rack placement, heat of the water,
type of bread, whether the house is humid.
This house is only humid in the bathroom,
after a long soak with the door closed. Or else,
in summer. But it's winter and a long time
before our flesh can rise and get sticky
in hands, on counters, in a proper resting place.

You Return with the Water: Indian Ocean Tsunami, 2004

I)

What was the apparatus that made your body stay in sleep?
It must have been an adaptation from life as a prey animal
standing in the turret. Your body was rigid
flogging against the sheets.
Your head often under the pillow,
arms squared in a military press.
But what was the weight you were holding?

We played the *Sleepytime Ocean* CD every night,
lullaby for a man whose night exhalations were sweet as apples.
Horses are able to sleep standing.
They doze and enter light sleep.
You were most vulnerable in bed;
your right eye open, responding to questions,
my cries against night-terror figures.

You talked me out of sleep,
asked about my dreams:
"Oh, you were tired of the Fruit People?
Why? They fed us lemons?
Tell me about the horse, about how I was a horse."

II)

We said good-bye before you left for Camp Atterbury,
your parents and I, in my best dress shirt,
after chicken finger dinners that later made us sick.
You begged me to finally fart for you.
We joked about sending me to Iraq,

to sit on the chests of enemies, gas their faces.
Enemies who dressed like my parents.

A few weeks later, after a small ice storm,
your phone call: they gave you Christmas.
I was on my empty campus, too cold to go home,
every day wearing my Rudolph the Reindeer robe.
I made you a cake. I put on lacy black underwear.
While I waited, rawing the base of my tailbone
with that cheap lace, 1000 miles of land slipped.
Waited 100 seconds. Slipped again.
A thousand dead. Tens of thousands dead. Maybe hundreds of.
People on a Thai beach said they saw large fish, sharks
on the sand. They took pictures of the water receding,
ran with bile rising faster than water,
feet slower than an ocean floor with its hackles up.

I turned it off. You missed the news those days,
and for over a year afterward.
Instead we made brittle snowballs,
slid on osteoporotic ice.
You in the green Battle Dress Uniform
they issued before your Desert Camouflage.
How do you train for Iraq in the Indiana woods,
in winter, without the random work of war?
I could simulate it by showing you the tsunami,
its multiple strikes,
its hours-long inundations.

We fell asleep, cake uneaten. You woke terrified,
telling me to get out, get out, the skunks in the forest
were coming to get me. I hunted for them
in your clothes, the leaves of your pants.
"Tell me about the forest,
about how I was a forest."

Sympathy for Satan

He's just a man, my mother says
now that men have come
verb-shifting, evading contexts,
covering themselves with ash
then calling themselves dark,
calling themselves devils.
They begin flowery discourses.
They sometimes enter a garden disguised as ferns.
They petition for possibilities beyond ease.
Satan asked questions he couldn't answer.
He unmoored himself, maybe forever,
because he dealt in knowledge, not rhetoric.
His punishment: silence,
confinement to the subjunctive.
"If only, if only," he says.
If only, if only leads to the devil.

A miniature man, vibrating in spit on my molars,
destroying silicone sealants in my ash-palette sleep.
He's a man, not capable of encouraging
honey palettes, not a sun that favors a window.
Not a mirror that bounces my own light onto my crown.
Just a man.

[In court, you submit to other humans.]
WHEREFORE, the petitioner prays:
I asked to dissolve the bonds now existing.
A miniature woman had worried the marrow of my heart-bone:
How long will you live a half-life,
half-life?

I believe in God's bounty.
He calls Himself *the Grateful.*

It lengthens the mind, to jump over narcissism
and find simple recognition: your Self in a great mirror
of your own construction.
I believe in God's bounty,
trust I'll ask Satan how it feels to court beings
who chose distance from ease,
with no rhetorical intent.
    He must talk through his teeth.
    His spit must vibrate between his teeth.
How it feels to deal entirely in regret,
his inheritance the first subjunctive construction:
If only.

What does it mean to pray for paradise now?
We don't wonder at our distance from greenness.
We could stand knee-deep in ferns and sob for another forest.
Is it possible God isn't angry?
Bewildered.
Certainly God could choose to go astray from Himself
and we'd ask: What is Your relationship to darkness? To light?

Inventory: Shrinkage

I lost my grip. / I balanced it on a piece of paper.
—Little Dragon

I can't turn my head   right,
salute the angel recording good deeds: *Hey.*
You must be idle lately.

"I'm missing my mind," I say.
My real laugh. My scream.

A gold compass gifted at birth.
A gold earring in the shape of an egg.
I lost my mother's pineapple necklace.
She lost her syrup scent.

My   mouth.
Every few months, I feel
it retreat. *At the corners.*

I can't tell the difference between
incense dust,
a rabbit pellet,
     Is it food or waste?
and the moon.
     It's all ash.

I lost my sense of direction.
I lost my sense of the sun.
I didn't know which way to pray
until an overweight housefly showed me.

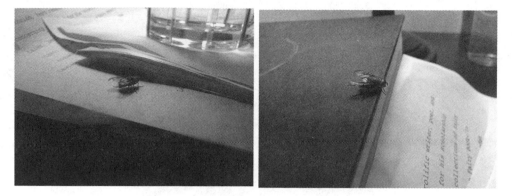

I forgot which burner I kept the kettle on.
My husband   kept   moving it,
so I lost my marriage, too.
Over thirty pounds,
and my linen slacks   but not the jacket;
my   cleavage;
I jiggled to my insteps when I chased buses.
my sense of time;
my ability to run after things;
a desire to set things   on fire.
I stole whistle cookies,
root beer.   Not men.
I lost my interest in stealing away.
I mean: being   stolen away.

       Once I climbed a pool-house wall
       to see water from above.
       I tore my fingers. They peel every few years.
       My mother says I made my fingers black *er.*
       At their joints. I started to climb a man
       but I think he was climbing, too.
       Like pools, I wonder if water
       looks better in blue eyes.
I made my heart an indoor inflatable,
and drop-kicked men who lingered.
We bounced   all over the place.

I jumped   off the top of my heart
onto them. Only I had access
to the second floor.

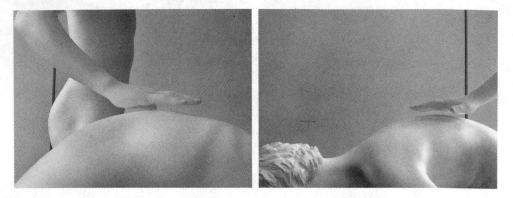

I'm losing my understanding
of metaphors. I blink
at allegory: *Of course Cain*
             had to one-up his brother.
             We all want our harvests accepted.
             Sometimes we cut down men.

My ability to cry   so the floor
springs pools   with no source. I blink.
Doorframes drip.   I blink.
The fridge leaks   three times,
stops when my landlord observes.
It must be quantum physics.
Is my home supposed to be my   self?
If so, they're turning off the water tomorrow.

When I look at the gristle on my heart,
I fraction. In a trinity-fold bathroom mirror,
especially at night, my recursive selves
are tinged green.
I'd like to call myself a   of ferns
but I've had difficulty with vocabulary
for living things,   thriving.

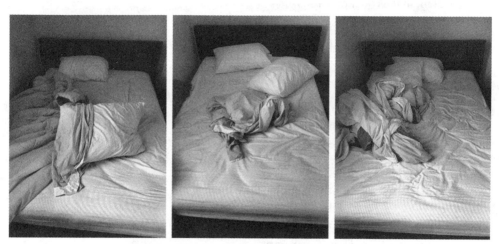

Do You Miss Waking Up Next to Someone?

Practice with Yearning Theorem: Tangents

I make room on the doormat
though no one is coming.
It's a hot night. I'll eat cool soup,
maybe out of the can. No,
garnish it: Are carrot shavings
good in butternut squash soup?
I take a photo, crop the bowl's chipped rim.
Maybe I'll send it to my siblings
to show them I'm living well.
I'm eating soup and salad
I couldn't buy at a restaurant most days.
I shower and sleep free from molesters.
I've paid my bills this month,
and washed my dishes
with my own two hands.
But am I grateful? Last night,
I tried to kill a moth. Two moths
sprang out of it, and split.
I didn't know moths made formations.
The night before that, I killed a moth,
got a paper towel to clean the wall,
and found another moth next to it.
I killed it, too. Why should I go on
killing moths? What have they done?
On the way home tonight,
I saw two pots of flowers
with fronds cascading from them.
Then a dog with his head,
forepaws outside the fence.
He needed a pat
but I recalled his barking,
his paws slapping the fence.
I wondered if this was the same dog.

On some hot nights, I remember
a poem about a restless woman
in a laundromat, her wetness.
At eighteen this was amusing.
Later, I read that rare plants
prime in laundromats
and understood her.
It's a hot night. End of summer.
A scratch on my nose burns
but I don't wash off my makeup
in case I go out.
Maybe I'll "get to go out,"
like a kid waiting at the back door,
her mother at the sink.
I kill yet another moth,
and consider leaving its body,
marker for cousins eating uneven holes
in the blooms of my favorite shawl.
I call it favorite after ruin.
I wore it to the conservatory
so it could visit siblings.
I'm concerned with families
—not the families of moths, apparently—
because I miss the one I came from,
and the one I don't have yet.
It's a hot night.
I'm aware of my wetness.
As a girl, I wore rosebud undershirts,
my chest poked out.
Relative women noted my posture,
said: *So, you're smelling yourself,*
and that, too, I understand only now.

The sea fell on my house

I was sweeping
and counting my cups
and rinsing my toothbrush
and bracing my hinges
when the sea fell on my house.
The sea fell on my house
when I'd braced for a straight-line wind.
The sea fell on my house
and I couldn't tell if it jumped on me
or me in it
but I was filled with the minerals
and matter
every beast and root on earth contain.
I couldn't tell if it jumped in me
or me in it
but I watched it fall out of my body
warm seawater from my body
onto the kitchen floor I'd just checked
for the earth-dust of winter
the brown dust of winter.

When you enter with it
don't say, "May."
Say, "Can. Can I?"
and I'll answer with a gesture.
Cover me with your body.
In the atmosphere between
our ribs: rain.
Rain containing the minerals
and salve
for every beast and root on earth.
Cover me and cover my cries.
My mouth a cave for the sea

to rush through
your tongue some urchin
assigned to live
off my minerals and matter.
Later, when delinquent
refuse to move, your belly at rest
your belly a palm on my belly.
Refuse to move until another train passes
and I'll say, "No," with a gesture.

The sea fell on my house.
The sky was paperwhite.
Just after noon.
An exact white.
Winter-salt crests and froth
on the sidewalks.
That should've been a warning
that the sea would fall.
The real one
not the sad sea of a snow mound
resisting spring.
The real one
fell on my house.

I couldn't tell if pressure
was at the front of my mind
or if my mind got stopped up
underwater.
The sea fell the sea fell the sea fell
on me and I'm at ease
and thirsty
and a figure is made known
a figure made from all the minerals
and matter
of his fellow beasts, the roots he eats.

We are thirsty and at ease
and falling asleep to the mineral scent
of our contribution to the sea.
We are thirsty and at ease
and the chalk and film of the sea
is dry on our thighs and fingers
and in the juvenile curve
under our lips.
We are thirsty and at ease
we are thirsty and at ease
we are thirsty and at ease
we are thirsty and at ease
and mindful of our salt
and thirsty and at ease
and resting
and assured of the yield we'll mine.

Sympathy for Eve

I wake with my right ankle in my right hand,
my right wrist in my left hand,
a tender, one-sided crucifixion,
pinning myself to sheets that seem wet,
5 a.m., always 5 a.m., and this time I think
there are dozens of dead bees bundled in the sheets,
their thoraxes and wings wet—with what?
Not even the air is moist.
Not even my hairline now that I've shaved
my temples and nape so I won't feel
a man's hands in that hair.
The way he turned from me
is so far outside my narrative
I decided to consider Eve,
the weight of what she could sense
but never witness:
complete devastation,
bees, and all their companions,
everything in the archive of earth
damp and beyond resurrection,
her foresight my only understanding
for the total dread I feel
against my arid longing,
that there are not even bees,
nothing but my belly against my thigh.

I imagine Eve, her automatic credibility,
her logic not yet accidental,
no one to review evidence against her,
no one to collect her papers
then read them generations later,
saying: "She lied, she was kind,
and not exacting at all. She wrote dozens

of letters to Satan asking after his heart,
under the pressure of his choices."

I consider Eve and the first time
Adam turned from her, after some argument
that certainly involved naming, valuing,
what it was for someone to spend a night
truly lonely while not alone, his sleeping back
to her, and her saying, "Well, I have my own
two arms, and the faculty to catalog:
tonight is the first night one hand
held tight the other." Or the first time
Adam attempted to lead her down a path
and she insisted it was a gorge,
its bottom water and snakes,
and she sat right where she'd been standing
until the sun set. By that time, she'd seen
enough refusals to know how to sit on sediment.
Or, the first time her very eyes
were a seasonal path, restricted by vines
and branches hard to strip or snap,
and her pupils said: "You may not enter
until the ground has thawed."
Adam paused and measured the snow at his feet.
Or the first time she was in his arms,
dizzy from too much sleep,
and relaxed further into him,
laid into him:
"We are not a biological imperative.
We were joined by the impulse for story."

II

Catastrophic Breakdown

The skin of every man
Horse Woman has ever loved
tastes like olives when she licks him,
like the sea thereafter.
There is nothing but the sea in the air.
There is nothing but the spice
that surrounds the sea in the air.
She is fully oriented to it.
There is no speed except her fullest.
She goes without hesitation.
She goes without food.
She goes without intention.
She goes with her nostrils and eyes
rimmed with her drying water,
white, the horizon and sun white,
the land mostly white,
she, black everywhere,
except the whites of her eyes,
which flare against exhaustion.
She goes with her ears
and the iron in her hooves
pointed to some shore,
no distinction between the wind
that enters, leaves her.
All the air is warm.
The sea smells warm.
There is nothing but the sea.
She goes in a land that is all salt,
salty marshes, later, white sands
that may be salt.
She goes with salt worrying her hooves.

She is still at the shore.

The water maintains a boundary.
She has salt in her heart; tastes it,
feels it pour out of her,
must her flank,
her riven and riven and riven heart
mended again and again
with her distilled desire
for the sea.

She finds some figure there,
indistinct from the water,
and becomes indistinct
from the scene,
her water or blood or the seawater
indistinct from each other.
Her riven and riven and riven heart,
raw from mending and desire,
recognizes its ability to break.

This breaks her legs.

She kneels to the sea
not to the figure, not yet.
The sea draws close enough
to put her forelock between its lips,
and she says to the figure there:
I submit to the sum and sea of you.
Haven't you always had me by my forelock?

Rebound Rapt (2016)

Devotional with Misheard Lyrics

There are so many boys from other realms
running in your hallway.
It's been a while since I heard spirits pacing,
chasing each other,
or little horses galloping in the sink,
whinnying in the walls.
We're in the habit of discussing nightmares,
a pair of sullen eyes.
Women who kill themselves twice.
I've met and disregarded them: *Your name?*
Your name again?
My heart is filed to a point. Heavy tip,
heavy blade, light handle, no sheath.
Unzip me and I'll be the same
but softer, lighter skinned underneath,
my face and feet the same color,
no blemishes, too much hair.
I feel like my force field is on high power.
I should drink more water.
Afternoon and evening pass, a sequence
of minor tremors in my wrists, forearms.
An algorithm reduces me to one sentence:
I am such a long day.
I'm often tired with my eleven o'clock.
I force a ten into a coin machine
and put all my silver monies
in my breast pocket. My heart is heavy
on the bottom again. When exiting,
I see a woman holding many bags.
She's tired, I think. Let me move, let me wait.
It's a reflection. I'm the woman
with Monday-night bags hanging off her wrists.
I smell like figs. *Boiled figs.*

In Somali, *timid* sounds like *date.*
Americans confuse dates and figs.
I can't eat twice with a man who does this.
You just want to be adored, you said,
then came next to worship over dinner,
rubbery plantains and two women
blushing and listening to you praise me:
If it were permissible to exalt
a mortal, you. You didn't say that.
I'm the most romantic man I know.
I'm simple only in this: I need two-armed hugs.
I sing in the street, small blasphemy
in the diaphragm's dome:
My lover's not human. Amen.
At the shrine of your light,
like a dog, like a dog.

All Bite the Bitten Dog

I held a mirror under my nose,
walked on the ceiling, hopped onto light covers,
stepped over doorframes, all rooms made new.
I'd wait when my breath fogged glass,
careful not to tilt the handle, glimpse my face.
I'd check my hair in glances, in the metal strip
at the side of the fridge.

I used my fingers to see the welts
from young, tender sticks, small rocks.
"Bleed!" a boy yelled but didn't wait
for the slow zipper of my flesh
to travel down my T-shirt.
"Look at all this sand! This paper!
These dead leaves!" my mother would say.
The water from my hair was often brown.
"I was playing. We were all playing."

An older boy raised a block of snow,
brought it down on my temple.
I could see my back door.
The frozen pavement showed sky,
and my eyes like raw chicken,
too pink from not crying.
There were friendly blue orbs, then nothing.
Then adults slowing but not stopping their cars,
though I'd have crawled to the road if they'd called me.
Then all the pink mouths. Fruit-punch mouths
showing evidence of every drink and sauce.

He left a little volcano near my eye,
clotted with ashen blood. So similar
to smoke-plant pods found in the burrs.

I covered it with my hair, pressed it away
with cold-water toilet paper.
These people can do whatever they want.
How long have they been doing whatever,
like I'm a hated dish towel, mildewed and carried in pinches.
They want to set me by the burner while they stand at the sink.

"Hey Niggerface, come here with that big forehead.
Let us rest our candle on it," the night the block's lights
went out. "Let us burn you. How long would it take
to burn you?" Their spit from behind fences when I passed:
it hung on chain links, thick and white
and full of the same something
that kept me from looking at my entire face at once.
They displayed dogs with bared teeth:
"Big Red busts basketballs."
A demonstration. The dog sent after me,
they screaming hysterically
when the animal stopped short.
The dog might snap its teeth for show.
What restrains it, what propels its owners.

After the Photograph of Emmett Till's Open Casket, 1955

I saw it with other little kids and we said, "Oh,
they made him into Play-Doh."
So every time I saw yellow
or mixed-up-colors Play-Doh,

I'd think of him. And whenever they talk
about him, I taste
its salt-sharp.
I hold a knot of it in my mouth since

Trayvon, after Jonatha Carr say my name—say my name'd
her professor, and asked
terrible questions, and whipped
her hair back and forth, she whipped her hair back and forth,

she whipped her hair back and forth.
After young Darius,
left outside for two hours
as they questioned his mother. The shooter

composed himself, his house,
and had his people over.
I taste Play-Doh

and dread seeing Emmett,
his whole and smiling body.
I see shadows of birds, branches, clouds over the moon,

in a clear sky. Or men, figures coming
toward me with a light.
They hold the light,
or, the light comes from their torsos.

I go to sleep hunted,
reaching for the KA-BAR
as if in the woods,
cursing, uncursing myself for taking apart the gun

and spreading its pieces because I had a bad feeling.
I got a bad feeling
about those night-terror figures
ever since I started thinking about Emmett.

I swore I'd never live in Money or Chicago
(because of the story about firefighters
letting black [houses] burn).
Now I wonder if I walk where he walked, and where his people are,

and if back then the boys of Bronzeville sometimes
looked like
a Biblical curse
befell them because they smile so shy and don't always

raise their eyes, weakening their chins by down-looking, as if
transfixed by
their shadows.
Black boys in my dreams, all tuned to the sun, waiting. (I smell

blood everywhere though the street is clean.) Their faces are
pennies,
smooth-molded
over their features, their faces Lincoln's face in profile.

I ask them, *Why, why this?*
They say,
We thought
it would be best. It's true,

they don't seem harmed.
Sunlight
on the pennies.
I rise with rancid tongue, belly,

think, maybe it wouldn't be so bad
if Emmett
appeared in his white shirt
and explained

some things. Mainly,
if it's as bad
as I think it is
when they finally get their hands on you.

In Which Christopher Robin Has an Incident

"You took your gun with you, just in case, as you always did,
and Winnie-the-Pooh went to a very muddy place that he knew of ..."

"[...] and rolled and rolled until he was black all over."

"*Ow!*" said Pooh.
"Did I miss?" you asked.

"I didn't hurt him when I shot him, did I?"
"Not a bit."

Double Consciousness I (2017)

Double Consciousness II (2017)

Double Consciousness III (2017)

Autocorrect

"Lynch whenever works best for you."
I mean, "Lunch." It's too late. So come
archived images of black bodies, hot.
I can tell they're hot, despite death,
by their skin. Later, I find a market
with the cheapest eggplants I've ever seen.
In perfect rows. I want their bitter skin,
the color a little like what's left after a burn,
or sunburn, especially where my arm bends.
Then, all I can talk about is history class,
social studies, how the teachers, even black
ones, don't tell you they're going to talk
about hot black bodies with balls and dicks
and maybe other meat stuffed in their mouths.
Why it's so important to see, without knowing
anything else about her, a black girl—woman—
who can tell with those full white skirts,
proned by batons or water or dogs.
When you're little and also wear good socks,
frilling socks with good shoes,
you think about the lace getting dirty, blood
on a white skirt, white socks, on shining black
or dark shoes. They should warn us
about their triggers.
What are the pictures for anyway?
White people (I can tell their skin
is dry), holding their hats, cameras,
each other. Squinting at a tree,
at the ground. *Why didn't each black
person kill a white person back.*
That's what I thought, looking at my textbook
or projector or Black History Month posters,

or the white students and the white teacher,
the few other blacks. I sweated a little.
Did I look hot? In a picture I'd have wet skin.
There, one could point a hundred years later
or less, an eggplant shine on my forehead.

NSFW

I want us to get off before this screen sleeps. I want to make a video
and play it on a loop, let it ruin someone's dinner.

I want to tell you I had a nightmare about Oscar Grant's murder
before it happened. I want you to believe me and turn me over
and over. Say: *This hole? This one?*
Cover them all. Fill my mouth so I stop tasting blood.

I want to dream we're miniature people
on a watermelon rind, rocking rocking.

I want to walk into a field at night, close our eyes
and mouths so the searchlights can't find us.
I want you to hold me in the grass, and later,
point at the drowned ants, our hides raw from mosquito bites.

I want you to recite your lineage.
Let us make formal prayers for the names we forget,
for the ones that history took.
Let us pray from the heart for the blood they took from us.

I want to give you my history of blood, of dirt, of police,
of teachers, of social workers, then laugh
with all our teeth showing.

I want you to time travel and make cards and bracelets
for the little girl who watched *A Time to Kill* and never healed.

I want you to braid my hair and really mess up.
I want you to braid my hair and make perfect parts.

I want to preside over the new Pan-African Congress.
Between sessions, daydream of my honeysuckle drying in your beard.
I want to feel you with my hand or foot under the welcome table.

I want us to *OOH!* like Michael and *YEOW!* like Prince.

I want you to bring me to incoherence. I want to keep you up
and ride into levity. I want to sing: *I get so weak in the knees*
off-key, my voice hoarse from screaming.

I want to sing all breakdowns and know their meanings.

I want us to get caught in one of Diana's closets, in her silks and satins.
I want to play our parents' records with eyes closed, smile and sway
like Stevie. I want us to procreate ourselves,
thereby knowing our folks, finally.

I want us to stay home as the others build Babel or turn to rubble.
I want to be Sheba revealing her ankles, ready to wade in water.
I want to wade in mine. I want to go until our biology stops us.
I want to almost go too far then stop
since Obamacare isn't as comprehensive as he'd hoped.

I want you to steal all my oils so you can smell like a shaman, too.
Let's wear linens and visit the pharaohs and scare people.

I want you to croon Wyclef's "911" and let me rub your back
and what shows when your pants are sagging.

I want to hum "A Change Is Gonna Come" with you in my mouth.

I want you against the hot and breathing grille of a truck or cop car.

I want you to cry falsetto tears if I start to leave you, better run to me
like the first seventeen seconds of Donny's "A Song for You."

I want to take a beat for our parents' pain,
then give them moody grandchildren.

I want to wake looking like Edward Scissorhands shaped my Afro.

I want you to minister to me in the morning,
pull us under the comforter so the neighbors and the walls
and our devices can't hear, and call each other by our secret names,
gasp: I can't breathe

I can't breathe

I can't breathe

I can't breathe

The Bee's Gospel

I enter a household wherein a woman uses stamps with blooms:
zinnia, aster, primrose. She adorns envelopes,
remembers her mother's destroyed marigolds
and grieves for them again.

At night a man puts his palm on her temple, then her crown,
unfolding meadows, and every fruit and root.
I sit on the headboard and wait for permission to enter.
It is an expanding paradise.
Every thing knows its relationship
to light, to darkness, pursues various means to the same ends,
and his hand contains the aliving spice
of a room full of palms.

He tells her she is the seasons.

He pursues a single lyric,
wears several musks at once.

In the morning she splits a dense fruit.
Within it are chambers, combs.
She extracts seeds on the table, spends songs cleaning them.

My guardian waits outside the window.

I like how this man looks when he offers things;
every object a gift: cup, washcloth, his scented
chest and temples. I don't know which one
is the queen, so I fly between them both.
And the backs of their necks are the same.
They are mirrors facing each other across a well-lit room.
I am in a frenzy.
I visit a cup whose color I can't resist:

summer sky after three nights without rain.
It contains a sweet fluid.
I don't know the name of this nectar.
It causes me to forget. I have to be near it,
on his knuckles, on his shoulders.
What does it want, she asks.
It doesn't know, he says.
What does it know of what humans made?
Then let him go and tell the others. Let him recite.
They try to kill me, not sincerely.
I drop from ceiling to floor until they, too, are exhausted.
She opens a window. I stay, parse their fragrances
as she parsed those seeds.
I want him to lie with her again,
show me multitudinous gardens.

My attendant can wait no longer.

I salute her bare right breast,
and watch her skin prickle
and her scalp flush,
and fly out.

III

"Think of Me as Your Mother"

For Mohammed el Gharani, a juvenile held at Guantánamo
for seven years

It's the Ides of March and I have too much longing. Lions and gales
replace speech. My mind breaks in a stone courtyard. It echoes as
if played from turrets. They admit me. They put my clothes in a bin
and search my skin for marks, cuts, and bruises; verify my eyes, hair,
toes, and knuckles are black. They remove the string from my hoodie
so I won't make a noose of it. I'm too tired to laugh about that. They
offer me rice. They say, *The rice is good,* and watch my face. They
think they know Africans. I say nothing. They give me medicine, two
kinds. I get free and yell: I'm BLACK! I'm black I'm black I'm black I'm
black I'm black I'm black I'm black I'm black I'm black and I've never
been to a wedding! After the medicine, I keep seeing my black and
yelling: WHAT IS THAT WHAT IS THAT WHAT IS THAT WHAT IS THAT?
They don't answer. A woman tells me to *Move it, bitch.* She's pretend-
ing a toy keyboard is a lie detector. I bump her hands and she has to
start all over. After the medicine, I can see my black and it can't stop
talking. It says: I'm not a demon. I'm a ghost. They're doing the wrong
rituals on me. They took inventory of my Keds, my Dickies, my ass,
but I'm still found without shoes or sheets. My chin stays bruised, and
a sore in my mouth makes me remember my wisdom teeth surgery
when I was seventeen and I had my first Muslim doctor, and he made
a mistake and gashed my cheek. To keep from crying, he bade me to
stop crying, even though I wasn't. They'd given me cackling gas. He
cooed: Everything will be ok, everything will be all right, everything
will be ok, everything will be all right. I screech: *I love myself!* in my
best Kendrick voice, spin like my feet are arabesque. They shoot me.
After that medicine, I stop rapping on tabletops and go to my bed.
The mattress receives me. I think of dark hair on a soft belly. The
blanket hugs me. I think of my baby sister sleeping on my mother's
back. I stay in my bed all day and miss all my prayers because the bed
says yes and yes. I want it to say no so its yes and yes is real. Can you

rape a bed by sleeping stubborn in it, even if its springs tell you to get out? Tell my mother to bring me some grease and my pik, to hide my hot hair curler in her skirt. I already know my hair better be laid when I lie in this therapist's face and tell her: *I just got confused.* They release me with three brown paper bags. All their handles break. They want me to look crazy in these streets but I just hum Badu in the parking lot and on the bus, break the high note: *Pack / light.* Every city built by the water is way too turnt. From Chicago to Istanbul, the thin caterwaul of stray felines, from midmorning to dusk. The geese that flew nowhere all winter holler in a knotted field at a devilish hour. Then there are gunshots. Police cracking ribs. The volume is up too high, too high in black ears. What do you do when a whole city is dog-whistling? A woman calls her young son *motherfucker.* His blink is blank. They face each other, hard-eyed. They have trouble translating the Quran into English. Hell is: the burning fire. Hell is: pain of mother losing child. In many places on earth, both definitions hold at the same time. I took my medicine, both kinds, and don't yell out the window: *RISE!* like dust in a Maya Angelou poem, and the voice of a kid reciting it. Rise like Fela's consorts when they were tossed out the compound windows, or like Maathai, or Mandela, or anyone whose knees or shoulders and skulls were clubbed in a dank prison. I wish I could take you into my belly. I think it's the only safe space for you. Come into my womb. You might find cinder blocks and mixed metal. You might find teeth and discreet ejaculations, and rancid tears and salvaged bits of scripture. Come into my placenta, my electric water via dream submarine. I will throw the key into the ocean. I am infinitely generative. You'll find your grandson guarding you. When you're ready to leave, he'll call to you: *All the best, goodbye goodbye.*

Boat Journey

Sunday afternoon on a city beach.
No sand, slabs of manufactured stone.
I watch two blondes, maybe sisters,
Inflate a raft. They use a bicycle pump.
One tries to assemble two paddles,
Gives up, puts them in her bag.
The one on the pump removes her top.
She has exerted herself into better posture.
Her breasts are larger than I expected.
I want to see if their tiny raft will hold them.
The clouds and current move north.
As they enter the water, Tony Allen warns
Against the boat journey: *Running away*
From a misery / Find yourself in a double misery.
I recall photos of British tourists in Greece
Frowning at refugees,
Greek children in gym class while hungry.
In the direction the raft floats, the sisters
Paddling with their hands, a planetarium.
I wonder if it houses a telescope capable
Of seeing the double misery on a Greek island.
Maybe its lens is too powerful.
The side of their raft reads EXPLORER.
Their soles are black. If you pay attention
To movies, white women have grimy soles.
I have seen black actresses with exquisite feet.
I recall my mother checking my socks
In the exam room before the doctor entered.
The sisters let their ponytails drag
In dubious lake water.
I'm not sure I hear these lyrics: *Even if*
They let you enter / They probably won't let you.
Even if they let you enter / The baron won't let you,

The baron won't let you.
I note their appearances,
Takeoff point. Just in case.
I doubt any of our thoughts converge.
What is it like to be so free?
To drift in water in a country you call
Your own. Unprepared because you can laugh
Into an official's face. Explain, offer no apology.

Practice with Yearning Theorem: Loci

Sometimes I visit Somalia via Google Maps. Information is spare.
It's a lesson in present time: not my parents' fortune, a comparison
of past and present images, a slide into prayers for the future.

I'm looking at a Catholic church damaged to grain. It's also defaced.

I wanted to document graffiti in Somalia. My parents weren't ready to let me visit. My father looked on my behalf in 2013. He said: I'm finding rubble.

I was on the edge of divorce but maybe only I knew that.

They're surprised when they find animals with compasses inside them, gulping for home. When fatigued, I visit the International Space Station.

A catastrophic separation: First, space between my joints. Then parts reduced to currents and less than that, stretching apart. I don't have physical language for it. If you report this form of pain they call it depression, or other sickness. My worst injuries were damaging my tailbone, several bad falls onto concrete or the edge of a step, into a dresser. I was leaping every time. This pain has no register.

My ex-husband would visit Iraq online, retrace the route he followed. This didn't seem legal. These tours were interminable. Probably his tour felt interminable. My lack of sympathy was a kernel between us. I hate uniforms, family reunion T-shirts. People all dressed the same, standing in a park.

He didn't agree not to talk about some things.

His most interesting story was about a field and stream near Abu Ghraib prison. I can't locate this green, this line, and should've paid better attention.

I was underwater in 2013. I'd look at the surface. Whatever I misheard was my own fault.

He told a story about firing tennis balls at an auto shop just beyond the prison. I confused his stories with news stories. (Was the bloody handprint never cleaned post-riot his recollection?) He said they aimed to the side of a lit cigarette hovering in the dark. They dented aluminum. It was a small thing, comparatively. But they scared someone taking a break after a long day. They dented his wall. No, it didn't matter if it was basically a shitty shed, it's his.

I visit countries in trouble. If there's water, I go there first. I look for green. Last, I look for airports, other infrastructure. Mogadishu, Aleppo, Baghdad.

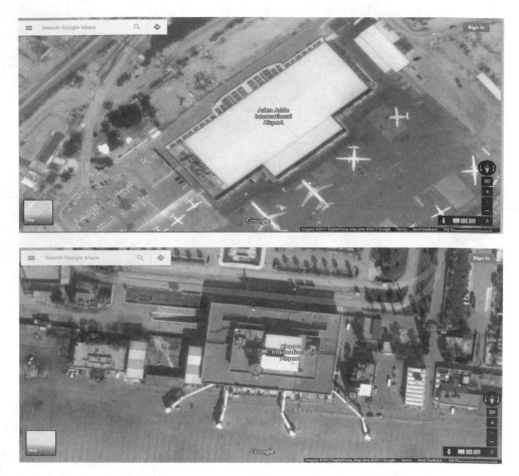

In Somali, *jab* means *break*, *fragment* but also *defeat* or *loss*. The meaning is closer to the motion between my joints and teeth and valves.

I sunder in a different language. My hope scatters in time. It's true I'm an alien here.

I used to say "after all" and mean "at the end," or "finally."
After all, America has broken my heart. This English is sufficient.

Introduction through Parables: Marwa

I was named after a well
my sister, too
after holy wells
distant from each other
we are distant from each other
our mother didn't intend it
war is the frantic wet nurse
running between us
we are both thirsty
we are all thirsty
there is no divine child
to make our waters holy
our waters heal no affliction
who would supplicate
at our bases, seek our waters
in parables
girls are never divine
only their mothers
but like Abraham
I ask God to show Himself
I ask in the plains
I ask in the desert
He answers me with light
He answers me with metal
tea with an iron flavor
we sell it town to town
migrants in our own wild bush
gunmetal sweat
weapon oil in the life-
and luck-lines of my palm
we traverse the land
we move with shadow
we are guided by water

I ask God to show Himself
a prophet quartered birds
and waited for God
yet another was given
a hoopoe that spoke
some have war birds
they, too, look
they, too, make reports
we live in a time
machines have emissaries
but like Abraham
it's not possible to destroy me
they try by fire and by sand
they try by metal and by verse
still I traverse my land
without a sister
with no family
not even a man
who no longer accepts
a hand on his chest
when frantic
myself, strange women
strange girls traverse
in this parable men and boys
attain godhood
they send war to run
hill to hill
well to well
war runs so fast
she loses a shoe
there is no holy child
war ran with empty arms
an empty shawl
when men and their boys
come to a frenzy

they can't submit to anything
no thing is a kindness
nothing is a kindness
don't touch me,
don't look at me,
with their whole persons
no one supplicates
to frantic gods
their command has no end
it can never become story
it can never become ritual

Landscape Genocide

My mother walked Liido Beach every morning when pregnant.
I know the mineral scent of saltwater wherever I am.
If the sun bakes the metal of earth, if my own damp scalp sweats,
if I hold my hennaed palms to my face.
I have said, "God. There is no god but God" into my metallic palms.
When my blood started, war started.
Ever since the war started, I dye a henna disk on each palm.
I refresh it when it browns, old blood. "God,"
into my mineral palms when the whole street was white sheets,
thin men digging graves night til dawn til night til dawn.
They paused for every single prayer.
An orb of light dragged me through a dim street, lifted me off my feet.
I shouted, "This is my light!" and held it tight against my belly.
I was still, beyond known stillness,
a gravity of my own, and still I didn't light the street.
The last thing my mother promised me was a photo of her,
five months pregnant, at the shore, backlit by the ocean.
"Go at dawn," she'd say. The water was warmest at dawn.
Girls went to the beach in whatever they were wearing,
even if they had school later. Their mothers couldn't keep them
from the water, from walking fully dressed into it.
There was nowhere to go but Liido.
The orb, a giant marble in my diaphragm, would float with me there.
There was nowhere to go but into the ocean.
Between this interior desert and the edge
of my known world, orange pekoe-tinted sand
marked with the heels and balls of firm and dazed feet.
Charred acacias facedown in the dust.
Succulents marking clusters of graves. Graves of people
and fruit-bearing trees. Bones of tall livestock,
the startling domes of camel ribs lit like a great hall
by the relentless sun. There is nowhere to go but the ocean.
Between here and its mineral scent, bones of people,

small and not small, bush lions and their young,
always litters of bones at the line between known
and wild worlds. Between here and Liido, the land
in full prostration. The only song, metallic. Shells,
or whole bullets underfoot, sometimes whole piles
at the edges and centers of towns put facedown
at night, at dawn, during afternoon prayer, at dusk.
Between here and Liido, the land and everything in it
in full submission to the mineral scent of our water
and blood and inability to cry anything,
not even "God! No god but God!" We go at dawn.

Parable for Refugees

seventeen common flies:
clustered: hallway: days:
they no longer fly through
the screen when ushered:
weak: to: from: light: real:
artificial: did they forget
the sun: fly toward faces:
some dead on a sill:
some walk: did they forget
how to fly: why don't they
go: one paces on a step: do
they wait for a shoe:
it averts them: goes: why die:
still: is it madness: the ones
who wait:

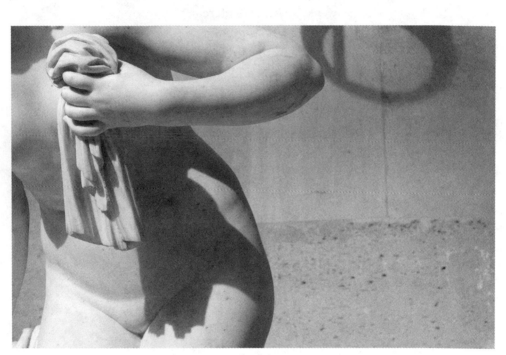

(2017)

Refusing Eurydice

Someone tells me the earth and everything in it
will belong to me if I catch the horizon before sundown.
I sprint, kicking up dust all the while.
It seems I run with everyone in the world
standing on my kidneys, eating my head.
What's that for? I ask.
I know how to eat my head.
The more I run, the more I feel
like a burned bit of rice fallen by the stove.
Someone is using my braids as bridle and whip.
It seems I'll run until my womb falls out of my body.
I look down a few times.
I run until sundown, and a bell sounds
from the four corners of earth.
I hum a workingwoman blues
and lie down with my eyes beating.
I sink into the ground,
down past stone and metal and water and fire.

Am I dead? I ask.

I slept so long, I went back to the place
souls wait for their forms.
In the schoolyard of my youth,
a peer and an elder tried to exorcise a shadow spirit.
They held me under my arms.
I was puking sludge and nightmaring ex-lovers,
sliding out the trash like chicken bones.
"There's still some shadow inside her," they said
and went away shaking their heads.
I went home. I tried to jump out the window.
I wanted to jump but didn't have anyone's name to scream.
I didn't ask God for a hug this time.

It was warm. I wanted to walk the streets naked
but didn't think I'd be left in peace.

Am I dead?
I keep saying:
I don't have to do shit but stay black and die!
Is dead what I'm doing? I was pretending ready.

I was breastfed only two months.
I have a poor memory of the sea
and am obsessed with water.
When pregnant,
my mother ate too much fish,
and sweet cakes and milk,
and cried on the beach.
My father said everything he ate had sand in it.
Halfway through a meal,
he'd find grains in the meat, in the salt,
on his glasses, which he'd take off
and rinse in water to avoid scratching them.
My mother's mother is buried in a dry land.
Her ghost would tire walking to the ocean.
Her grave is marked with a bowl of water and a succulent.
Her daughters pledged to build her a well,
and lay green carpets in a holy house.
I promised my mother I'd write a poem about ablutions.
I haven't done it because I don't know
which part needs washing first.
Am I dead?
There are bodies all around me.
A swarm of flies takes custody of the pile of corpses.
Get up, an African witch from Atlanta says.
There is no Hades. You don't get to choose death.
You're an immigrant, not a refugee.
You've flown to and fro over the ocean in peace since birth.

There are many who look like you—down, in the water,
down, where Solomon's jinns found gems, and deeper.
They've murmured in the sludge and oil of primordial time,
throwing up pearls and other stones.

Thrive, says an African witch from Atlanta.
I rise, my mind looming with fly-song.
Go to your sisters, the witch says.
I rouse two women. We walk in a huddle,
covering each other with our funk.
We bleed freely and eat,
inhale a metallic scent from our temples,
from behind our knees, and higher up our legs.
We eat near men who are fasting.
The men's eyes and lungs suck the scent
of the flesh we women carry, the flesh we eat.
Fruit flies circle our plates, our waists.
The witch lights incense and smokes our hair,
the white linen we wear faceup in the grass,
watching billow topped by billow,
our hems blowing around our knees.
Once rested, the witch demands a spell for flourishing:
Recite reason to live, she says.
Though your tongue makes errors,
say yea or say yeah,
and it is still devotion.

My sisters exhale light, a mist.
I start with my origins:
I am Ladan,
who knows her mother,
and her mother's mothers
twenty generations back.
I am a lion born in a house of fire.
I am a Leo born to a woman with burned forearms.

I am not permitted to ask her how she got them.
I tell myself she bore them delivering me.
I am Ladan, whom my father wanted to name after a holy well.
My mother insisted they call me *well-being* instead.
I have been asleep a long time.
I was playing patty-cake with my shadow,
and others' shadows for too long.
I died chasing the horizon, and got up anyway.
I am here to inherit the earth and everything in it.
I want what every being has a right to,
and then more than that.
I possess one compass, which is my soul,
and it shall never err.
May my voice penetrate
as a steed in battle penetrates an enemy mass.
I have restored myself
and am searching for a green man,
a man who lays leaves as he walks.
I have recovered myself
and am looking for my unborn child,
whom the witches ask me to greet.

*The green man will approach your kingdom
in writing,* the witch says.
Do not be ashamed to test men.
The green one will warm your flesh in his palms,
then lick you from behind
until you find your own water under your feet.
Now go tell your troubles to a tree.
I scream grievances at an acacia until it's damp / I'm parched.
I leave my sisters and go to a good man,
the wings of a pregnant housefly beating my eyelashes.
I oil my palms and rub his brown to bark.
They took me to a forest floor
of broken mouths, I tell him.

They took me to an alley
flooded with drool, he tells me.
I watched my words fall into a well, I say.
The Word flew, birds rendered
off the edge of composition, he says.
I ask him to show me a hill of black children in repose.
To loom me fine linen.
I'm hard as a tree, he says. You flood my sod.
Yes, I say. *You're so hard, and I take it and make it look easy.*
I have been low. I am on high.
Record my relief.
Let us wade in our water.
We walk, asleep, exhaling pollen.

We go to the place between dreams.
It's buttressed by ancestors
who tell us they're proud.
They interrupt our waking motions
to remind us they're proud.
Let us go to the place between dreams.
If you're too worried about women
running shoeless away from whatever
or whoever pursues them,
ready to slam a door on their ankles,
go to the place between dreams,
where no woman has to run with a broken ankle
and a heart that's a blade in a washer,
tumbling on and bleeding into a stomach
that receives this blood as acid.
Go to the place between dreams,
where your flank shimmers in the moonlight
or a streetlight of your pleasure.
I am not a woman who has had to run with a broken ankle.
Praise God and praise the feet that meet steps
and cracks with confidence.

Go to the place between dreams, where all the light is yours.
Even if it looks like headlights or streetlights or floodlights
held by whatever or whoever pursues you,
the light is yours. Even if it has to drag you at first,
hold it against your beating stomach and gurgling heart.
Go to the place between dreams,
where a woman's mild voice looms.
She offers instruction you can't yet hear.
Follow her. She has never run with a broken ankle,
or with her thigh shimmering in any light not her own.
Go to the place between dreams.
The building and grounds
are covered by forms pacing
or reclining or sitting.

Enter a marble room.
It's full of steam. It's filled with forms.
Each is naked.
Some are covered in fine hair.
Some shaved everything except a patch behind their knees
or just under their tailbones.
There is no hesitation. There is no imperfection.
Sit and imagine the pleasure of sitting in your own lap,
your daughter sitting in your lap.
Sitting between your aged mother's legs,
with your daughter in your lap.
Lie on hot marble chestfirst.
Listen to voices murmur and echo.
You're inside your heart.
Listen to your sighing.
You didn't know your voice was so musical,
why it pleased the ones who love you,
repulsed the ones confused by you.
Feel your voice on top of your teeth,
vibrating in the spit on top of and between your teeth.

Let your voice be food.
Let it line your gums where they meet your cheeks.
Let its particles linger at the back of your tongue,
a muscular member, that thing capable
of true penetration, soft but never flaccid.
May your thoughts be muscular, too.
May you make so many things,
your tendons pulse, aching for work.
On earth, they worked women so hard,
their wombs fell out while walking.
Remember this lying bellyfirst on hot marble.
Bless their wombs.
Bless the womb fallen from a woman who had to keep walking.
Lie on hot marble flankfirst.
You carried the pain of your humiliated mother
on the outer curve of each shoulder blade.
Leave all of that hallway and stairway and bathtub moaning
here on this hot marble. It cannot reenter
in defiance of your illuminated flank.
Finger the scar that runs dark from bellybutton to clitoris.
Remember you are not a woman who was cut.
Remember your mother said: *Not my daughters*
and the elder women said: *Okay.*
You do not fear any examination or detention or operation.
Obviously God has removed some thing from you,
and waits for you to go to the place past dreaming
so you can ask. The address you are seeking
is the place past dreaming, and when you go there,
God will return the flesh or dimness
removed so you can be birthed into the place
where you are now, lying flankfirst
and fingering your flesh with all your faculties intact.

This is a congregation refusing Eurydice.
We refuse death by spells.

We refuse death by attack.
We refuse death by falling,
and we refuse death in depressions.
We refuse the spirits that attempt oppression,
and we refuse the spirits that attempt possession.
We refuse humans who call themselves gods,
who try to graft hellfire onto our bodies,
and raise columns of fire in our yards.
We are looking for better myths.
We are tired of falling
and finding ourselves underfoot.
We are searching the earth
for images that draw parables.
We left the serpents underfoot in peace
and refuse their bites.
We refuse death by discourse.
We refuse death by exile.
We refuse death by falling,
and we refuse death in depressions.
We are looking for a better myth.
We've only been looking since Eve.

Notes

"Half-Life" includes a line from the Wikipedia article "Biological Half-Life." https://en.wikipedia.org/wiki/Biological_half-life.

"Devotional with Misheard Lyrics" references misheard lyrics from "Take Me to Church," performed by Hozier and written by Andrew Hozier-Byrne, 2013.

"After the Photograph of Emmett Till's Open Casket, 1955" references lyrics from "Say My Name," performed by Destiny's Child and written by Fred Jerkins III, Kelly Rowland, LaShawn Ameen Daniels, Rodney Jerkins, Beyoncé Knowles, LaTavia Roberson, and LeToya Luckett, 1999; and "Whip My Hair," performed by Willow Smith and written by Ronald Jackson and Janae Luann Ratliff, 2010.

"NSFW" references lyrics from "Weak," performed by SWV and written by Brian Morgan, Larry Troutman, Roger Troutman, and Shirley Murdock, 1992.

"'Think of Me as Your Mother'" takes its title from an interrogation session. The final lines of this poem quote fellow detainee Shaker Aamer upon Mohammed el Gharani's release, as reported in "Bringing Guantánamo to Park Avenue" by Laurie Anderson, originally published in the *New Yorker,* September 23, 2015, https://www.newyorker.com/culture/cultural-comment/bringing-guantanamo-to-park-avenue.

This poem references lyrics from "I," performed by Kendrick Lamar and written by O'Kelly Isley, Christopher Jasper, Ernie Isley, Rudolph Isley, Ronald Isley, Marvin Isley, and Kendrick Duckworth, 2015; and "Bag Lady," performed by Erykah Badu and written by Erykah Badu and André Young, Nathaniel Hale, Ricardo Brown, and Isaac Hayes, 2000.

This poem was commissioned by the *Tea Project,* an activist art act created by Aaron Hughes and Amber Ginsburg, http://tea-project.org.

"Boat Journey" references misheard lyrics from "Boat Journey," written and performed by Tony Allen, 2014.

"Refusing Eurydice": an excerpt from this poem appeared in issue 4 of *Let's Panic* magazine, 2018. It includes a line from "Another Way to Die" by Haruki Murakami and translated by Jay Rubin—"A huge swarm of flies had already taken custody of the pile of corpses"— originally published in the *New Yorker* on January 20, 1997, https://www.newyorker.com/magazine/1997/01/20/another-way-to-die.

Image Credits

Sculpture details shown in "Inventory: Shrinkage" are from *Huck and Jim,* © Charles Ray. Used courtesy of Matthew Marks Gallery.

Illustrations and text excerpted in "*In Which* Christopher Robin Has an Incident" are from "*In Which* We Are Introduced to Winnie-the-Pooh and Some Bees, and the Stories Begin," in *Winnie-the-Pooh* by A. A. Milne, illustrated by Ernest H. Shepard (New York: EP Dutton & Company, 1926).

Photographs of the church front in "Practice with Learning Theorem: Loci" are by Boris Kester, www.traveladventures.org. Used with permission.

Map images in "Practice with Learning Theorem: Loci" are by Google, © 2017 by DigitalGlobe; map data © 2017 by Google.

Photograph of mosque in "Practice with Learning Theorem: Loci" is by Mohamed Al-hadi. Used with permission.

Sculpture shown in untitled photograph, *(2017),* is *Diane au bain* by Christophe-Gabriel Allegrain, 1778.

All other images © Ladan Osman.

Acknowledgments

Thanks to the editors of the following publications in which these poems, sometimes in different versions, first appeared:

Academy of American Poets's Poem-a-Day: "Boat Journey"

The Baffler: "Autocorrect"

Callaloo: "Landscape Genocide"

Columbia Poetry Review: "The sea fell on my house"

Cordite Poetry Review: "Introduction through Parables: Marwa"

Fanzine: "Inventory: Shrinkage"

Ninth Letter: "Catastrophic Breakdown," "You Return with the Water: Indian Ocean Tsunami, 2004"

Pop-Up Magazine: "After the Photograph of Emmett Till's Open Casket, 1955"

Prachya Review: "Practice with Yearning Theorem: Tangents"

Prairie Schooner: "The Bee's Gospel"

Puerto del Sol: "Half-Life," "Sympathy for Satan"

The Rumpus: "All Bite the Bitten Dog," "Devotional with Misheard Lyrics," "*In Which* Christopher Robin Has an Incident," "NSFW"

Wasafiri: "Parable for Refugees"

Washington Square Review: "Sympathy for Eve," "'Think of Me as Your Mother'"

I am grateful to the Lannan Foundation and Cave Canem for their generous support of my work.

Thanks to my editor, Erika Stevens, for her precision and kindness, as well as the staff at Coffee House Press. For their contributions, thanks to: Oumou Diallo, Louvre Museum, Charles Ray, Mohamed Al-hadi, Boris Kester, John Penney, and Izzy Penney. Light on light to my first readers: my siblings, Donika Kelly, Joelle Mercedes, Cristina Correa, Airea D. Matthews, Keith S. Wilson, Ted Kooser, Brigit Pegeen Kelly, and Joe Penney.

LITERATURE
is not the same thing as
PUBLISHING

Coffee House Press began as a small letterpress operation in 1972 and has grown into an internationally renowned nonprofit publisher of literary fiction, essay, poetry, and other work that doesn't fit neatly into genre categories.

Coffee House is both a publisher and an arts organization. Through our *Books in Action* program and publications, we've become interdisciplinary collaborators and incubators for new work and audience experiences. Our vision for the future is one where a publisher is a catalyst and connector.

Funder Acknowledgments

Coffee House Press is an internationally renowned independent book publisher and arts nonprofit based in Minneapolis, MN; through its literary publications and *Books in Action* program, Coffee House acts as a catalyst and connector—between authors and readers, ideas and resources, creativity and community, inspiration and action.

Coffee House Press books are made possible through the generous support of grants and donations from corporations, state and federal grant programs, family foundations, and the many individuals who believe in the transformational power of literature. This activity is made possible by the voters of Minnesota through a Minnesota State Arts Board Operating Support grant, thanks to the legislative appropriation from the Arts and Cultural Heritage Fund. Coffee House also receives major operating support from the Amazon Literary Partnership, the Jerome Foundation, McKnight Foundation, Target Foundation, and the National Endowment for the Arts (NEA). To find out more about how NEA grants impact individuals and communities, visit www.arts.gov.

Coffee House Press receives additional support from the Elmer L. & Eleanor J. Andersen Foundation; the David & Mary Anderson Family Foundation; Bookmobile; Fredrikson & Byron, P.A.; Dorsey & Whitney LLP; the Fringe Foundation; Kenneth Koch Literary Estate; the Knight Foundation; the Matching Grant Program Fund of the Minneapolis Foundation; Mr. Pancks' Fund in memory of Graham Kimpton; the Schwab Charitable Fund; Schwegman, Lundberg & Woessner, P.A.; the U.S. Bank Foundation; and VSA Minnesota for the Metropolitan Regional Arts Council.

The Publisher's Circle of Coffee House Press

Publisher's Circle members make significant contributions to Coffee House Press's annual giving campaign. Understanding that a strong financial base is necessary for the press to meet the challenges and opportunities that arise each year, this group plays a crucial part in the success of Coffee House's mission.

Recent Publisher's Circle members include many anonymous donors, Suzanne Allen, Patricia A. Beithon, the E. Thomas Binger & Rebecca Rand Fund of the Minneapolis Foundation, Andrew Brantingham, Robert & Gail Buuck, Dave & Kelli Cloutier, Louise Copeland, Jane Dalrymple-Hollo, Mary Ebert & Paul Stembler, Kaywin Feldman & Jim Lutz, Chris Fischbach & Katie Dublinski, Sally French, Jocelyn Hale & Glenn Miller, the Rehael Fund-Roger Hale/Nor Hall of the Minneapolis Foundation, Randy Hartten & Ron Lotz, Dylan Hicks & Nina Hale, William Hardacker, Randall Heath, Jeffrey Hom, Carl & Heidi Horsch, the Amy L. Hubbard & Geoffrey J. Kehoe Fund, Kenneth & Susan Kahn, Stephen & Isabel Keating, Julia Klein, the Kenneth Koch Literary Estate, Cinda Kornblum, Jennifer Kwon Dobbs & Stefan Liess, the Lambert Family Foundation, the Lenfestey Family Foundation, Sarah Lutman & Rob Rudolph, the Carol & Aaron Mack Charitable Fund of the Minneapolis Foundation, George & Olga Mack, Joshua Mack & Ron Warren, Gillian McCain, Malcolm S. McDermid & Katie Windle, Mary & Malcolm McDermid, Sjur Midness & Briar Andresen, Maureen Millea Smith & Daniel Smith, Peter Nelson & Jennifer Swenson, Enrique & Jennifer Olivarez, Alan Polsky, Marc Porter & James Hennessy, Robin Preble, Alexis Scott, Ruth Stricker Dayton, Jeffrey Sugerman & Sarah Schultz, Nan G. & Stephen C. Swid, Kenneth Thorp in memory of Allan Kornblum & Rochelle Ratner, Patricia Tilton, Joanne Von Blon, Stu Wilson & Melissa Barker, Warren D. Woessner & Iris C. Freeman, and Margaret Wurtele.

For more information about the Publisher's Circle and other ways to support Coffee House Press books, authors, and activities, please visit www.coffeehousepress.org/pages/support or contact us at info@coffeehousepress.org.

This project was made possible
through generous support from

THE FRINGE FOUNDATION

Somali-born poet and essayist **Ladan Osman** is the author of *The Kitchen-Dweller's Testimony* (University of Nebraska Press 2015), winner of the Sillerman First Book Prize, and the author of the chapbook *Ordinary Heaven*, which appeared in the box set *Seven New Generation African Poets* (Slapering Hol Press 2014).

Exiles of Eden was designed by Bookmobile Design & Digital Publisher Services. Text is set in Kepler Std.